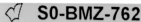
MIYAMOTO MUSASHI

THE BOOK OF FIVE RINGS

Translated by
THOMAS CLEARY

Unabridged

SHAMBHALA
Boston & London
1994

Shambhala Publications, Inc.
Horticultural Hall
300 Massachusetts Avenue
Boston, Massachusetts 02115
www.shambhala.com

15   14   13   12   11   10   9   8

Printed in Canada
∞ This edition is printed on acid-free paper that meets
the American National Standards institute Z39.48 Standard.
Distributed in the United States by Random House, Inc.,
and in Canada by Random House of Canada Ltd

See page 152 for Library of Congress
Cataloging-in-Publication data.

Cover art: Blockprint by Kuniyoshi. Reproduced courtesy
of Ronin Gallery, New York.

This edition does not include Yagyu Munenori's *Family
Traditions on the Art of War,* which can be found in the
Shambhala Dragon Edition.

THE BOOK OF
FIVE RINGS

CONTENTS

TRANSLATOR'S PREFACE

THE JAPANESE WORD *shin-ken* means "real sword," but it is now more generally used in a metaphorical sense. In common parlance, to do something with a real sword means to do it with utmost earnestness. To have an attitude proper to a real sword means to be deadly serious. *Shin-ken shō-bu,* literally a contest with real swords, means something done in deadly earnest.

This molecule of linguistic anthropology hints at a very good reason why the Japanese are as persistent and skilled as they are at survival and adaptation. Through centuries of cultural training under the martial rule of the samurai, the

Japanese are generally able to experience and address virtually anything as a life-and-death situation.

This book shows how they do it.

TRANSLATOR'S
INTRODUCTION

THE BOOK OF FIVE RINGS is one of the most important texts on conflict and strategy emerging from the Japanese warrior culture. Originally written not only for men-at-arms, it is explicitly intended to symbolize processes of struggle and mastery in all concerns and walks of life.

The Book of Five Rings was written in 1643 by Miyamoto Musashi, undefeated dueler, masterless samurai, and independent teacher. Musashi was a professional man-at-arms born into a long tradition of martial culture that had ultimately come to dominate the entire body of Japanese polity and society. His insights are relevant not only to members of the ruling military caste, but also to leaders in other professions, as well as people in search of individual mastery in whatever their chosen path.

The Book of Five Rings is written in Japanese, rather than the literary Chinese customary in elite bureaucratic, religious, and intellectual circles in Japan at that time. The Japanese in which it is written, furthermore, is relatively uncomplicated and quite free of the subtle complexities of classical high court Japanese. Although the crudity of Musashi's syntax and morphology make for clumsy reading, nevertheless the basic simplicity and deliberate clarity of the work makes it accessible to a wide and varied audience.

The rise and empowerment of the samurai class in Japan may be seen in the two terms used to refer to its members, *samurai* and *bushi*. The word *samurai* comes from the Japanese verb *saburau,* which means "to serve as an attendant." The word *bushi* is Sino-Japanese and means "armed gentry." The word *samurai* was used by other social classes, while the warriors referred to themselves by the more dignified term *bushi*.

The original samurai were attendants of nobles. In time their functions expanded to the administration, policing, and defense of the vast estates of the nobles, who were mostly absentee landlords. Eventually the samurai demanded and won a greater share of the wealth and political power that the nobles had called their own. Ultimately the military paragovernment of the Shōguns, known as the Bakufu, or Tent Government, overshadowed the imperial organization and dominated the whole country.

Musashi lived in the founding era of the third Tent Government, which lasted from the beginning of the seventeenth century through the middle of the nineteenth century. While inheriting the martial traditions of its predecessors, this third Tent Government differed notably in certain respects.

The first Tent Government was established in eastern Japan near the end of the twelfth century and lasted for nearly one hundred and fifty years. The warriors of this time were descendants of noble houses, many of whom had honed their martial skills for generations in warfare against the Ainu people in eastern Japan. As the Tent Government was seated in Kamakura, a small town near modern Tōkyō, this period of Japanese history is commonly called the Kamakura era.

The second Tent Government supplanted the first in 1338. The warrior class had expanded and become more differentiated by this time, with lesser and thinner genealogical ties to the ancient aristocracy.

The Shōguns of this period established their Tent Government in Kyōto, the old imperial capital, and tried to establish high culture among the new samurai elite. This period of Japanese history is commonly called the Ashikaga era, after the surname of the Shōguns, or the Muromachi era, after the name of the outlying district of Kyōto in which the Tent Government was located.

To understand Japanese history and culture, it is essential to realize that no government ever united the whole country until the Meiji Restoration of 1868. The imperial government had always ruled the whole land in theory, but never in fact. The imperial house had never really been more than a center of powerful factions, competing with other powerful factions. Even when everyone recognized the ritual and political status of the emperor in theory, direct imperial rule only reached a portion of the land.

As this is true of the imperial house, so is it also true of the military governments. The reign of the Shōguns was always complicated and mitigated by the very nature of the overall Japanese power structure. The rule of the Kamakura Tent Government was not absolute, that of the Muromachi Tent Government even less. Separatism, rivalry, and civil warfare marked the fifteenth and sixteenth centuries.

By this time, known as the era of the Warring States, the way of war was open to anyone who could obtain arms by any means. Lower-class samurai rose up to overthrow the upper-class samurai, and Japan was plunged into chaos. It was not until the latter part of the sixteenth century that a series of hegemons emerged with strategy and power sufficient to move dramatically toward unification. The third Tent Government was built on the achievements of those hegemons.

Within the context of traditional Japanese society, the founder of the third Shogunate was an upstart and a usurper. Aware of this, he set out to establish a most elaborate system of checks and controls to ensure the impossibility of such an event ever occurring again. Moving his capital again to eastern Japan, away from the heartland of the ancient aristocracy and imperial regime, the new Shōgun disarmed the peasants and disenfranchised the samurai class, removing all warriors from the land and settling them in castle towns. This period of Japanese history is commonly known as the Tokugawa era, after the surname of the Shōguns, or the Edo period, after the name of the new capital city, now called Tōkyō.

Tokugawa Japan was divided into more

than two hundred baronies, which were classified according to their relationship to the Tokugawa clan. The barons were controlled by a number of methods, including regulation of marriage and successorship, movement of territories, and an elaborate hostage system. The baronies were obliged to minimize their contingents of warriors, resulting in a large number of unemployed samurai known as *rōnin,* or wanderers.

Many of the disenfranchised samurai became schoolteachers, physicians, or priests. Some continued to practice martial traditions, and to teach them to others. Some became hooligans and criminals, eventually to constitute one of the most serious social problems of the later Tokugawa period. Certain characteristics of *The Book of Five Rings* stem from the fact that Miyamoto Musashi was a masterless samurai pursuing a career as a dueler and an independent teacher of martial arts.

More properly titled in English *The Book of Five Spheres,* Miyamoto Musashi's work is devoted to the art of war as a purely pragmatic enterprise. Musashi decries empty showmanship and commercialization in martial arts, focusing attention on the psychology and physics of lethal assault and decisive victory as the essence of warfare. His scientifically aggressive, thoroughly ruthless approach to military science, while not universal among Japanese martialists, represents a highly concentrated characterization of one particular type of samurai warrior.

Although a vast body of legend grew up around his dramatic exploits, little is known for certain about the life of Miyamoto Musashi. What he says of himself in *The Book of Five Rings* is the primary source of historical information. He killed a man for the first time when he was thirteen years old, for the last time when he was twenty-nine. At some point he apparently gave up using a real sword but continued to inflict mortal wounds on his adversaries until the end of his fighting career.

The last three decades of Musashi's life were spent refining and teaching his military science. It is said that he never combed his hair, never took a bath, never married, never made a home, and never fathered children. Although he also took up cultural arts, as indeed he recommends to everyone, Musashi himself bascially pursued an ascetic warrior's path to the end.

Born into strife, raised in mortal combat, ultimately witness to a transition to peacetime polity on a scale unprecedented in the history of his nation, Miyamoto Musashi abandoned an ordinary life to exemplify and hand on two essential elements of ancient martial and strategic traditions.

The first of these basic principles is keeping inwardly calm and clear even in the midst of violent chaos; the second is not forgetting about the possibility of disorder in times of order. As a warrior of two very different worlds, a world of war and a world of peace, Musashi was obliged to practice both of these fundamental aspects of the warrior's way in a most highly intensified manner, lending to his work a keenness and a ferocity that can hardly be surpassed.

Ever since the samurai took power in Japan, centuries before Musashi was born, Buddhists had been trying to civilize and educate the warriors. This does not mean that the samurai caste in general was successfully imbued with Buddhist enlightenment, or even with a Buddhist spirit. One prominent reason for this was that the Buddhists were kept busy, not only trying to civilize the samurai, but also trying to clean up after them and their follies. Buddhism was burdened with the tasks of burying the dead, taking in and raising the many children orphaned by war or poverty or cast off as bastards, and sheltering abused and abandoned wives.

In the relationship between Zen and the samurai, therefore, the teacher should not be assessed by the level of the student. If martial arts were really considered the highest form of study in Japan, as has been suggested by some apologists, Zen masters would have been the students of the warriors, and not the other way around.

The prolonged domination of Japan by the martial caste was an anomaly in human affairs, as reflected by its discord with both native Japanese and greater East Asian sociopolitical ideals. Because of the way martial rule was established by power, it was fated to bend social and philosophical ideals to its own purposes, rather than submit itself completely to the judgment and guidance of the traditional religions and philosophies it professed to uphold.

THE BOOK OF
FIVE RINGS

PREFACE

THE SCIENCE of martial arts called the Individual School of Two Skies is something that I have spent many years refining. Now, wishing to reveal it in a book for the first time, I have ascended Mount Iwato in Higo province of Kyūshū. Bowing to Heaven, paying respects to Kannon, I face the Buddha. I am Shinmen Musashi no Kami, Fujiwara no Genshin, a warrior born in the province of Harima, now sixty years old.

I have set my mind on the science of martial arts since my youth long ago. I was thirteen years old when I had my first duel. On that occasion I won over my opponent, a martial artist named Arima Kihei of the New School of Accuracy. At sixteen years of age I beat a powerful martial artist called Akiyama of Tajima province. When I was twenty-one, I went to the capital city and met martial artists from all over the country. Although I engaged in numerous duels, never did I fail to attain victory.

After that, I traveled from province to province, meeting martial artists of the various schools. Although I dueled more than sixty times, never once did I lose. That all took place between the time I was thirteen years old and the time I was twenty-nine.

When I had passed the age of thirty and reflected on my experiences, I realized that I had not been victorious because of consummate attainment of martial arts. Perhaps it was because I had an inherent skill for the science and had not deviated from natural principles. It may also have been due to shortcomings in the martial arts of other schools. In any case, I subsequently practiced day and night in order to attain an even deeper principle, and spontaneously came upon the science of martial arts. I was about fifty years old at that time.

Since then I have passed the time with no science into which to inquire. Trusting in the advantage of military science, as I turn it into the sciences of all arts and skills, I have no teacher in anything.

Now, in composing this book, I have not borrowed the old sayings of Buddhism or Confucianism, nor do I make use of old stories from military records or books on military science. With Heaven and Kannon for mirrors, I take up the brush and begin to write, at 4:00 A.M. on the night of the tenth day of the tenth month, 1643.

The Earth Scroll

MARTIAL ARTS are the warrior's way of life. Commanders in particular should practice these arts, and soldiers must also know this way of life. In the present day there are no warriors with certain knowledge of the way of martial arts.

First let us illustrate the idea of a way of life. Buddhism is a way of helping people, Confucianism is a way of reforming culture. For the physician, healing is a way of life; a poet teaches the art of poetry. Others pursue fortune-telling, archery, or various other arts and crafts. People practice the ways to which they are inclined, developing individual preferences. Few people are fond of the martial way of life.

First of all, the way of warriors means familiarity with both cultural and martial arts. Even if they are clumsy at this, individual warriors should strengthen their own martial arts as much as is practical in their circumstances.

People usually think that all warriors think about is being ready to die. As far as the way of death is concerned, it is not limited to warriors. Mendicants, women, farmers, and even those below them know their duty, are ashamed to neglect it, and resign themselves to death; there is no distinction in this respect. The martial way of life practiced by warriors is based on excelling others in anything and everything. Whether by victory in an individual duel or by winning a battle with several people, one thinks of serving the interests of one's employer, of serving one's own interests, of becoming well known and socially established. This is all possible by the power of martial arts.

Yet there will be people in the world who think that even if you learn martial arts, this will not prove useful when a real need arises. Regarding that concern, the true science of martial arts means practicing them in such a way that they will be useful at any time, and to teach them in such a way that they will be useful in all things.

ON THE SCIENCE OF MARTIAL ARTS

In China and Japan, practitioners of this science have been referred to as masters of martial arts. Warriors should not fail to learn this science.

People who make a living as martial artists these days only deal with swordsmanship. The priests of the Kashima and Kantori shrines in Hitachi province have established such schools, claiming their teachings to have been transmitted from the gods, and travel around from province to province passing them on to people; but this is actually a recent phenomenon.

Among the arts and crafts spoken of since ancient times, the so-called art of the advantage has been included as a craft; so once we are talking about the art of the advantage, it cannot be limited to swordsmanship alone. Even swordsmanship itself can hardly be known by considering only how to win by the art of the sword alone; without question it is impossible to master military science thereby.

As I see society, people make the arts into commercial products; they think of themselves as commodities, and also make implements as items of commerce. Distinguishing the superficial and the substantial, I find this attitude has less reality than decoration.

The field of martial arts is particularly rife with flamboyant showmanship, with commercial popularization and profiteering on the part of both those who teach the science and those who study it. The result of this must be, as someone said, that "amateuristic martial arts are a source of serious wounds."

Generally speaking, there are four walks of life: the ways of the knight, the farmer, the artisan, and the merchant.

First is the way of the farmer. Farmers prepare all sorts of agricultural tools and spend the years constantly attending to the changes in the four seasons. This is the way of the farmer.

Second is the way of the merchant. Those who manufacture wine obtain the various implements required and make a living from the profit they gain according to quality. Whatever the business, merchants make a living from the profits they earn according to their particular status. This is the way of the merchant.

Third, in regard to the warrior knight, that path involves constructing all sorts of weapons and understanding the various properties of weapons. This is imperative for warriors; failure to master weaponry and comprehend the specific advantages of each weapon would seem to indicate a lack of cultivation in a member of a warrior house.

Fourth is the way of the artisan. In terms of the way of the carpenter, this involves skillful construction of all sorts of tools, knowing how to use each tool skillfully, drawing up plans correctly by means of the square and the ruler, making a living by diligent practice of the craft.

These are the four walks of life, of knights, farmers, artisans, and merchants. I will illustrate the science of martial arts by likening it to the way of the carpenter.

The carpenter is used as a metaphor in reference to the notion of a house. We speak of aristocratic houses, military houses, houses of the arts; we speak of a house collapsing or a house continuing; and we speak of such and such a tradition, style, or "house." Since we use the expression "house," therefore, I have employed the way of the master carpenter as a metaphor.

The word for carpenter is written with characters meaning "great skill" or "master plan." Since the science of martial arts involves great skill and master planning, I am writing about it in terms of comparison with carpentry.

If you want to learn the science of martial arts, meditate on this book; let the teacher be the needle, let the student be the thread, and practice unremittingly.

LIKENING THE SCIENCE OF MARTIAL ARTS TO CARPENTRY

As the master carpenter is the overall organizer and director of the carpenters, it is the duty of the master carpenter to understand the regulations of the country, find out the regulations of the locality, and attend to the regulations of the master carpenter's own establishment.

The master carpenter, knowing the measurements and designs of all sorts of structures, employs people to build houses. In this respect, the master carpenter is the same as the master warrior.

When sorting out timber for building a house, that which is straight, free from knots, and of good appearance can be used for front pillars. That which has some knots but is straight and strong can be used for rear pillars. That which is somewhat weak yet has no knots and looks good is variously used for door sills, lintels, doors, and screens. That which is knotted and crooked but nevertheless strong is used thoughtfully in consideration of the strength of the various members of the house. Then the house will last a long time.

Even knotted, crooked, and weak timber can be made into scaffolding, and later used for firewood.

As the master carpenter directs the journeymen, he knows their various levels of skill and gives them appropriate tasks. Some are assigned to the flooring, some to the doors and screens, some to the sills, lintels, and ceilings, and so on. He has the unskilled set out floor joists, and gets those even less skilled to carve wedges. When the master carpenter exercises discernment in the assignment of jobs, the work progresses smoothly.

Efficiency and smooth progress, prudence in all matters, recognizing true courage, recognizing different levels of morale, instilling confidence, and realizing what can and cannot be reasonably expected—such are the matters on the mind of the master carpenter. The principle of martial arts is like this.

THE SCIENCE OF MARTIAL ARTS

Speaking in terms of carpentry, soldiers sharpen their own tools, make various useful implements, and keep them in their utility boxes. Receiving instructions from a master carpenter, they hew pillars and beams with adzes, shave floors and shelving with planes, even carve openwork and bas relief. Making sure the measurements are correct, they see to all the necessary tasks in an efficient manner; this is the rule for carpentry. When one has developed practical knowledge of all the skills of the craft, eventually one can become a master carpenter oneself.

An essential habit for carpenters is to have sharp tools and keep them whetted. It is up to the carpenter to use these tools masterfully, even making such things as miniature shrines, bookshelves, tables, lamp stands, cutting boards, and pot covers. Being a soldier is like this. This should be given careful reflection.

Necessary accomplishments of a carpenter are avoiding crookedness, getting joints to fit together, skillful planing, avoiding abrasion, and seeing that there is no subsequent warping.

If you want to learn this science, then take everything I write to heart and think it over carefully.

On the Composition of This Book in Five Scrolls

Distinguishing five courses, in order to explain their principles in individual sections, I have written this book in five scrolls, entitled Earth, Water, Fire, Wind, and Emptiness.

In the Earth Scroll is an outline of the science of martial arts, the analysis of my individual school. The true science cannot be attained just by mastery of swordsmanship alone. Knowing the small by way of the great, one goes from the shallow to the deep. Because a straight path levels the contour of the earth, I call the first one the Earth Scroll.

Second is the Water Scroll. Taking water as the basic point of reference, one makes the mind fluid. Water conforms to the shape of the vessel, square or round; it can be a drop, and it can be an ocean.

Water has the color of a deep pool of aquamarine. Because of the purity of water, I write about my individual school in this scroll.

When you attain certain discernment of the principles of mastering swordsmanship, then, when you can defeat one opponent at will, this is tantamount to being able to defeat everyone in the world. The spirit of overcoming others is the same even if there are thousands or tens of thousands of opponents.

The military science of commanders is to construe the large scale from the small scale, like making a monumental icon from a miniature model. Such matters are impossible to write about in detail; to know myriad things by means of one thing is a principle of military science. I write about my individual school in this Water Scroll.

Third is the Fire Scroll. In this scroll I write about battle. Fire may be large or small, and has a sense of violence, so here I write about matters of battle. The way to do battle is the same whether it is a battle between one individual and another or a battle between one army and another. You should observe reflectively, with overall awareness of the large picture as well as precise attention to small details.

The large scale is easy to see; the small scale is hard to see. To be specific, it is impossible to reverse the direction of a large group of people all at once, while the small scale is hard to know because in the case of an individual there is just one will involved and changes can be made quickly. This should be given careful consideration.

Because the matters in this Fire Scroll are things that happen in a flash, in martial arts it is essential to practice daily to attain familiarity, treating them as ordinary affairs, so the mind remains unchanged.

17

Therefore I write about contest in battle in this Fire Scroll.

Fourth is the Wind Scroll. The reason I call this scroll the Wind Scroll is that it is not about my individual school; this is where I write about the various schools of martial arts in the world. As far as using the word *wind* is concerned, we use this word to mean "style" or "manner" in speaking of such things as ancient style, contemporary style, and the manners of the various houses; so here I write definitively about the techniques of the various schools of martial arts in the world. This is "wind." Unless you really understand others, you can hardly attain your own self-understanding.

In the practice of every way of life and every kind of work, there is a state of mind called that of the deviant. Even if you strive diligently on your chosen path day after day, if your heart is not in accord with it, then even if you think you are on a good path, from the point of view of the straight and true, this is not a genuine path. If you do not pursue a genuine path to its consummation, then a little bit of crookedness in the mind will later turn into a major warp. Reflect on this.

It is no wonder that the world should consider the martial arts to consist solely of swordsmanship. As far as the principles and practices of my martial arts are concerned, this is a distinctly different matter. I write about other schools in this Wind Scroll in order to make the martial arts of the world known.

Fifth is the Emptiness Scroll. The reason this scroll is entitled Emptiness is that once we speak of "emptiness," we can no longer define the inner depths in terms of the surface entryway. Having attained a principle, one detaches from the principle; thus one has spontaneous independence in the science of martial arts and naturally attains marvels: discerning the rhythm when the time comes, one strikes spontaneously and naturally scores. This is all the way of emptiness. In the Emptiness Scroll I have written about spontaneous entry into the true Way.

ON NAMING THIS INDIVIDUAL SCHOOL "TWO SWORDS"

The point of talking about two swords is that it is the duty of all warriors, commanders and soldiers alike, to wear two swords. In olden times these were called *tachi* and *katana,* or the great sword and the sword; nowadays they are called *katana* and *wakizashi,* or the sword and the side arm. There is no need for a detailed discussion of the business of warriors wearing these two swords. In Japan, the way of warriors is to wear them at their sides whether they know anything about them or not. It is in order to convey the advantages of these two that I call my school Two Swords in One.

As for the spear, the halberd, and so on, they are considered extra accoutrements; they are among the tools of the warrior.

For beginners in my school, the real thing is to practice the science wielding both swords, the long sword in one hand and the short sword in the other. When your life is on the line, you want to make use of all your tools. No warrior should be willing to die with his swords at his side, without having made use of his tools. However, when you hold something with both hands, you cannot wield it freely both right and left; my purpose is to get you used to wielding the long sword with one hand.

With large weapons such as the spear and the halberd, there is no choice; but the long and short swords are both weapons that can be held in one hand.

The trouble with wielding a long sword with both hands is that it is no good on horseback, no good when running hurriedly, no good on marshy ground, muddy fields, stony plains, steep roads, or crowded places.

When you have a bow or a spear in your left hand, or whatever other weapon you are wielding, in any case you use the long sword with one hand; therefore, to wield the long sword with both hands is not the true way.

When it is impossible to strike a killing blow using just one hand, then use two hands to do it. It should not require effort. Two Swords is a way to learn to wield the long sword in one hand, whose purpose is first to accustom people to wielding the long sword in one hand.

The long sword seems heavy and unwieldy to everyone at first, but everything is like that when you first take it up: a bow is hard to draw, a halberd is hard to swing. In any case, when you become accustomed to each weapon, you become stronger at the bow, and you acquire the ability to wield the long sword. So when you attain the power of the way, it becomes easy to handle.

To swing the long sword with great velocity is not the right way, as will be made clear in the second section, the Water Scroll. The long sword is to be wielded in spacious places, the short sword in confined spaces; this is the basic idea of the way to begin with.

In my individual school, one can win with the long sword, and one can win with the short sword as well. For this reason, the precise size of the long sword is not fixed. The way of my school is the spirit of gaining victory by any means.

It is better to wield two swords than one long sword when you are battling a mob all by yourself; it is also advantageous when taking prisoners.

Matters such as this need not be written out in exhaustive detail; myriad things are to be inferred from each point. When you have mastered the practice of the science of martial arts, there will be nothing you do not see. This should be given careful and thorough reflection.

ON KNOWING THE PRINCIPLES OF THE WORDS "MARTIAL ARTS"

In this path, someone who has learned to wield the long sword is customarily called a martial artist in our society. In the profession of martial arts, one who can shoot a bow well is called an archer, while one who has learned to use a gun is called a gunner. One who has learned to use a spear is called a lancer, while one who has learned to use a halberd is called a halberdier.

If we followed this pattern, one who has learned the way of the sword would be called a longswordsman and a sidearmsman. Since the bow, the gun, the spear, and the halberd are all tools of warriors, all of them are avenues of martial arts. Nevertheless, it is logical to speak of martial arts in specific reference to the long sword. Because society and individuals are both ordered by way of the powers of the long sword, therefore the long sword is the origin of martial arts.

When you have attained the power of the long sword, you can singlehandedly prevail over ten men. When it is possible to overcome ten men singlehandedly, then it is possible to overcome a thousand men with a hundred, and to overcome ten thousand men with a thousand. Therefore, in the martial arts of my individual school, it is the same for one man as it is for ten thousand; all of the sciences of warriors, without exception, are called martial arts.

As far as paths are concerned, there are Confucians, Buddhists, tea connoisseurs, teachers of etiquette, dancers, and so on. These things do not exist in the way of warriors. But even if they are not your path, if you have wide knowledge of the ways, you encounter them in everything. In any case, as human beings, it is essential for each of us to cultivate and polish our individual path.

ON KNOWING THE ADVANTAGES OF WEAPONS IN MARTIAL ARTS

In distinguishing the advantages of the tools of warriors, we find that whatever the weapon, there is a time and situation in which it is appropriate.

The side arm, or short sword, is mostly advantageous in confined places, or at close quarters, when you get right up close to an opponent. The long sword generally has appropriate uses in any situation. The halberd seems to be inferior to the spear on a battlefield. The spear is the vanguard, the halberd the rear guard. Given the same degree of training, one with a spear is a bit stronger.

Both the spear and the halberd depend on circumstances; neither is very useful in crowded situations. They are not even appropriate for taking prisoners; they should be reserved for use on the battlefield. They are essential weapons in pitched battle. If you nevertheless learn to use them indoors, focusing attention on petty details and thus losing the real way, they will hardly prove suitable.

The bow is also suitable on the battle-field, for making strategic charges and retreats; because it can be fired rapidly at a moment's notice from the ranks of the lancers and others, it is particularly good for battle in the open fields. It is inadequate, however, for sieging a castle, and for situations where the opponent is more than forty yards away.

In the present age, not only the bow but also the other arts have more flowers than fruit. Such skills are useless when there is a real need.

Inside castle walls, nothing compares to a gun. Even in an engagement in the open fields, there are many advantages to a gun before the battle has begun. Once the ranks have closed in battle, however, it is no longer adequate.

One virtue of the bow is that you can see the trail of the arrows you shoot, which is good. An inadequacy of the gun is that the path of the bullets cannot be seen. This should be given careful consideration.

As for horses, it is essential for them to have powerful stamina and not be temperamental.

Speaking in general terms of the tools of the warrior, one's horse should stride grandly, one's long and short swords should cut grandly, one's spear and halberd should penetrate grandly, and one's bow and gun should be strong and accurate.

You should not have any special fondness for a particular weapon, or anything else, for that matter. Too much is the same as not enough. Without imitating anyone else, you should have as much weaponry as suits you. To entertain likes and dislikes is bad for both commanders and soldiers. Pragmatic thinking is essential.

On Rhythm in Martial Arts

Rhythm is something that exists in everything, but the rhythms of martial arts in particular are difficult to master without practice.

Rhythm is manifested in the world in such things as dance and music, pipes and strings. These are all harmonious rhythms.

In the field of martial arts, there are rhythms and harmonies in archery, gunnery, and even horsemanship. In all arts and sciences, rhythm is not to be ignored.

There is even rhythm in being empty.

In the professional life of a warrior, there are rhythms of rising to office and rhythms of stepping down, rhythms of fulfillment and rhythms of disappointment.

In the field of commerce, there are rhythms of becoming rich and rhythms of losing one's fortune.

Harmony and disharmony in rhythm

occur in every walk of life. It is imperative to distinguish carefully between the rhythms of flourishing and rhythms of decline in every single thing.

The rhythms of the martial arts are varied. First know the right rhythms and understand the wrong rhythms, and discern the appropriate rhythms from among great and small and slow and fast rhythms. Know the rhythms of spatial relations, and know the rhythms of reversal. These matters are specialties of martial science. Unless you understand these rhythms of reversal, your martial artistry will not be reliable.

The way to win in a battle according to military science is to know the rhythms of the specific opponents, and use rhythms that your opponents do not expect, producing formless rhythms from rhythms of wisdom.

With the science of martial arts of my individual school outlined above, by diligent practice day and night the mind is naturally broadened; transmitting it to the world as both collective and individual military science, I write it down for the first time in these five scrolls entitled Earth, Water, Fire, Wind, and Emptiness.

For people who want to learn my military science, there are rules for learning the art:

1. Think of what is right and true.
2. Practice and cultivate the science.
3. Become acquainted with the arts.
4. Know the principles of the crafts.
5. Understand the harm and benefit in everything.
6. Learn to see everything accurately.
7. Become aware of what is not obvious.
8. Be careful even in small matters.

9. Do not do anything useless.

Generally speaking, the science of martial arts should be practiced with such principles in mind. In this particular science, you can hardly become a master of martial arts unless you can see the immediate in a broad context. Once you have learned this principle, you should not be defeated even in individual combat against twenty or thirty opponents.

First of all, keep martial arts on your mind, and work diligently in a straightforward manner; then you can win with your hands, and you can also defeat people by seeing with your eyes. Furthermore, when you refine your practice to the point where you attain freedom of the whole body, then you can overcome people by means of your body. And since your mind is trained in this science, you can also overcome people by means of mind. When you reach this point, how could you be defeated by others?

Also, large-scale military science is a matter of winning at keeping good people, winning at employing large numbers of people, winning at correctness of personal conduct, winning at governing nations, winning at taking care of the populace, winning at carrying out customary social observances. In whatever field of endeavor, knowledge of how to avoid losing out to others, how to help oneself, and how to enhance one's honor is part of military science.

The Water Scroll

T HE HEART of the individual Two Skies school of martial arts is based on water; putting the methods of the art of the advantage into practice, I therefore call this the Water Scroll, in which I write about the long sword system of this individual school.

It is by no means possible for me to write down this science precisely as I understand it in my heart. Yet, even if the words are not forthcoming, the principles should be self-evident. As for what is written down here, every single word should be given thought. If you think about it in broad outlines, you will get many things wrong.

As for the principles of martial arts,

although there are places in which I have written of them in terms of a duel between two individuals, it is essential to understand in terms of a battle between two armies, seeing it on a large scale.

In this way of life in particular, if you misperceive the path even slightly, if you stray from the right way, you fall into evil states.

The science of martial arts is not just a matter of reading these writings. Taking what is written here personally, do not think you are reading or learning, and do not make up an imitation; taking the principles as if they were discovered from your own mind, identify with them constantly and work on them carefully.

State of Mind in Martial Arts

In the science of martial arts, the state of mind should remain the same as normal. In ordinary circumstances as well as when practicing martial arts, let there be no change at all — with the mind open and direct, neither tense nor lax, centering the mind so that there is no imbalance, calmly relax your mind, and savor this moment of ease thoroughly so that the relaxation does not stop its relaxation for even an instant.

Even when still, your mind is not still; even when hurried, your mind is not hurried. The mind is not dragged by the body, the body is not dragged by the mind. Pay attention to the mind, not the body. Let there be neither insufficiency nor excess in your mind. Even if superficially weakhearted, be inwardly stronghearted, and do not let others see into your mind. It is essential for those who are physically small to know what it is like to be large, and for those who are physically large to know what it is like to be small; whether you are physically large or small, it is essential to keep your mind free from subjective biases.

Let your inner mind be unclouded and open, placing your intellect on a broad plane. It is essential to polish the intellect and mind diligently. Once you have sharpened your intellect to the point where you can see whatever in the world is true or not, where you can tell whatever is good or bad, and when you are experienced in various fields and are incapable of being fooled at all by people of the world, then your mind will become imbued with the knowledge and wisdom of the art of war.

There is something special about knowledge of the art of war. It is imperative to master the principles of the art of war and learn to be unmoved in mind even in the heat of battle.

Physical Bearing in Martial Arts

As for physical appearance, your face should not be tilted downward, upward, or to the side. Your gaze should be steady. Do not wrinkle your forehead, but make a furrow between your eyebrows. Keep your eyes unmoving, and try not to blink. Narrow your eyes slightly. The idea is to keep a serene expression on your face, nose straight, chin slightly forward.

The back of the neck should be straight, with strength focused in the nape. Feeling the whole body from the shoulders down as one, lower the shoulders, keep the spine straight, and do not let the buttocks stick out. Concentrate power in the lower legs, from the knees down through the tips of the feet. Tense the abdomen so that the waist does not bend.

There is a teaching called "tightening the wedge," which means that the abdomen is braced by the scabbard of the short sword in such a manner that the belt does not loosen.

Generally speaking, it is essential to make your ordinary bearing the bearing you use in martial arts, and make the bearing you use in martial arts your ordinary bearing. This should be given careful consideration.

FOCUS OF THE EYES IN MARTIAL ARTS

The eyes are to be focused in such a way as to maximize the range and breadth of vision. Observation and perception are two separate things; the observing eye is stronger, the perceiving eye is weaker. A specialty of martial arts is to see that which is far away closely and to see that which is nearby from a distance.

In martial arts it is important to be aware of opponents' swords and yet not look at the opponents' swords at all. This takes work.

This matter of focusing the eyes is the same in both small- and large-scale military science.

It is essential to see to both sides without moving the eyeballs.

Things like this are hard to master all at once when you're in a hurry. Remember what is written here, constantly accustom yourself to this eye focus, and find out the state where your eye focus does not change no matter what happens.

GRIPPING THE LONG SWORD

In wielding the long sword, the thumb and forefinger grip lightly, the middle finger grips neither tightly nor loosely, while the fourth and little fingers grip tightly. There should be no slackness in the hand.

The long sword should be taken up with the thought that it is something for killing opponents. Let there be no change in your grip even when slashing opponents; make your grip such that your hand does not flinch. When you strike an opponent's sword, block it, or pin it down, your thumb and forefinger alone should change somewhat; but in any case you should grip your sword with the thought of killing.

Your grip when cutting something to test your blade and your grip when slashing in combat should be no different, gripping the sword as you would to kill a man.

Generally speaking, fixation and binding are to be avoided, in both the sword and the hand. Fixation is the way to death, fluidity is the way to life. This is something that should be well understood.

ON FOOTWORK

In your footwork, you should tread strongly on your heels while allowing some leeway in your toes. Although your stride may be long or short, slow or fast, according to the situation, it is to be as normal. Flighty steps, unsteady steps, and stomping steps are to be avoided.

Among the important elements of this science is what is called complementary stepping; this is essential. Complementary stepping means that you do not move one foot alone. When you slash, when you pull back, and even when you parry, you step right-left-right-left, with complementary steps. Be very sure not to step with one foot alone. This is something that demands careful examination.

FIVE KINDS OF GUARD

The five kinds of guard are the upper position, middle position, lower position, right-hand guard, and left-hand guard. Although the guard may be divided into five kinds, all of them are for the purpose of killing people. There are no other kinds of guard besides these five.

Whatever guard you adopt, do not think of it as being on guard; think of it as part of the act of killing.

Whether you adopt a large or small guard depends on the situation; follow whatever is most advantageous.

The upper, middle, and lower positions are solid guards, while the two sides are fluid guards. The right and left guards are

for places where there is no room overhead or to one side. Whether to adopt the
right or left guard is decided according to
the situation.

What is important in this path is to realize that the consummate guard is the
middle position. The middle position is
what the guard is all about. Consider it in
terms of large-scale military science: the
center is the seat of the general, while following the general are the other four
guards. This should be examined carefully.

THE WAY OF THE LONG SWORD

To know the Way of the long sword means
that even when you are wielding your
sword with two fingers, you know just
how to do it and can swing it easily.

When you try to swing the long sword
fast, you deviate from the Way of the long
sword, and so it is hard to swing. The idea

45

is to swing the sword calmly, so that it is easy to do.

When you try to swing a long sword fast, the way you might when using a fan or a short sword, you deviate from the Way of the long sword, so it is hard to swing. That is called "short sword mincing" and is ineffective for killing a man with a long sword.

When you strike downward with the long sword, bring it back up in a convenient way. When you swing it sideways, bring it back sideways, returning it in a convenient way. Extending the elbow as far as possible and swinging powerfully is the Way of the long sword.

PROCEDURES OF
FIVE FORMAL TECHNIQUES

First Technique

In the first technique, the guard is in the middle position, with the tip of the sword pointed at the opponent's face. When you close ranks with the opponent, and the opponent strikes with the long sword, counter by deflecting it to the right. When the opponent strikes again, you hit the point of his sword back up; your sword now having bounced downward, leave it as it is until the opponent strikes again, whereupon you strike the opponent's hands from below.

These five formal techniques can hardly be understood just by writing about them. The five formal techniques are to be practiced with sword in hand. By means of these five outlines of swordplay, you will know my science of swordplay, and the techniques employed by opponents will also be evident. This is the point of telling you that there are no more than five guards in the Two Sword method of swordsmanship. Training and practice are imperative.

Second Technique

In the second technique of swordplay, the guard is in the upper position, and you strike the opponent at the very same time as the opponent tries to strike you. If your sword misses the opponent, leave it there for the moment, until the opponent strikes again, whereupon you strike from below, sweeping upward. The same principle applies when you strike once more.

Within this technique are various states of mind and various rhythms. If you practice the training of my individual school by means of what lies within this technique, you will gain thorough knowledge of the five ways of swordplay and will be able to win under any circumstances. It requires practice.

Third Technique

In the guard of the third technique, the sword is held in the lower position; with a feeling of taking matters in hand, as the opponent strikes, you strike at his hands from below. As you strike at his hands, the opponent strikes again; as he tries to knock your sword down, bring it up in rhythm, then chop off his arms sideways after he has struck. The point is to strike an opponent down all at once from the lower position just as he strikes. The guard with the sword in the lower position is something that is met with both early on and later on in the course of carrying out this science; it should be practiced with sword in hand.

Fourth Technique

In the guard of the fourth technique, the sword is held horizontally to the left side, to hit the opponent's hands from below when he tries to strike. When the opponent tries to knock down your sword as it strikes upward from below, block the path of his sword just like that, with the idea of hitting his hands, and cut diagonally upward toward your shoulder. This is the way to handle a long sword. This is also the way to win by blocking the path of the opponent's sword if he tries to strike again. This should be considered carefully.

Fifth Technique

In the fifth procedure, the sword is held horizontally to your right side. When you note the location of the opponent's attack, you swing your sword from the lower side diagonally upward into the upper guard position, then slash directly from above. This is also essential for expertise in the use of the long sword. When you can wield a sword according to this technique, then you can wield a heavy long sword freely.

These five formal techniques are not to be written down in detail. To understand the use of the long sword in my school, and also generally comprehend rhythms and discern opponents' swordplay techniques, first use these five techniques to develop your skills constantly. Even when fighting with opponents, you perfect the use of the long sword, sensing the minds of opponents, using various rhythms, gaining victory in any way. This requires careful discernment.

ON THE TEACHING OF HAVING
A POSITION WITHOUT A POSITION

Having a position without a position, or a guard without a guard, means that the long sword is not supposed to be kept in a fixed position. Nevertheless, since there are five ways of placing the sword, the guard positions must follow along. Where you hold your sword depends on your relationship to the opponent, depends on the place, and must conform to the situation; wherever you hold it, the idea is to hold it so that it will be easy to kill the opponent.

Sometimes the upper guard position is lowered a bit, so that it becomes the middle position, while the middle guard position may be elevated a bit, depending on the advantage thereof, so that it becomes the upper position. At times the lower guard position is also raised a bit, to become the middle position. The two side-guard positions may also be moved some-what toward the center, depending on where you are standing vis-à-vis your opponent, resulting in either the middle or lower guard position.

In this way, the principle is to have a guard position without a position. First of all, when you take up the sword, in any case the idea is to kill an opponent. Even though you may catch, hit, or block an opponent's slashing sword, or tie it up or obstruct it, all of these moves are opportunities for cutting the opponent down. This must be understood. If you think of catching, think of hitting, think of blocking, think of tying up, or think of obstructing, you will thereby become unable to make the kill. It is crucial to think of everything as an opportunity to kill. This should be given careful consideration.

In large-scale military science, the arraying of troops is also a matter of positioning. Every instance thereof is an opportunity to win in war. Fixation is bad. This should be worked out thoroughly.

STRIKING DOWN AN OPPONENT IN A SINGLE BEAT

Among the rhythms used to strike an opponent, there is what is called a single beat. Finding a position where you can reach the opponent, realizing when the opponent has not yet determined what to do, you strike directly, as fast as possible, without moving your body or fixing your attention.

The stroke with which you strike an opponent before he has thought of whether to pull back, parry, or strike is called the single beat. Once you have learned this rhythm well, you should practice striking the intervening stroke quickly.

The Rhythm of the Second Spring

The rhythm of the second spring is when you are about to strike and the opponent quickly pulls back or parries; you feint a blow, and then strike the opponent as he relaxes after tensing. This is the stroke of the second spring.

It will be very difficult to accomplish this stroke just by reading this book. It is something that you understand all of a sudden when you have received instruction.

Striking without Thought and without Form

When your opponent is going to strike, and you are also going to strike, your body is on the offensive, and your mind is also on the offensive; your hands come spontaneously from space, striking with added speed and force. This is called striking without thought or form, and is the most important stroke. This stroke is encountered time and time again. It is something that needs to be learned well and refined in practice.

THE FLOWING WATER STROKE

The flowing water stroke is used when you are going toe to toe with an opponent, when the opponent tries to pull away quickly, dodge quickly, or parry your sword quickly: becoming expansive in body and mind, you swing your sword from behind you in an utterly relaxed manner, as if there were some hesitation, and strike with a large and powerful stroke.

Once you have learned this stroke, it is certainly easy to strike. It is essential to discern the opponent's position.

THE CHANCE HIT

When you launch an offensive and the opponent tries to stop it or parry it, you strike at his head, hands, and feet with one stroke. Striking wherever you can with one swoop of the long sword is called the chance hit. When you learn this stoke, it is one that is always useful. It is something that requires precise discernment in the course of dueling.

THE SPARK HIT

The spark hit is when your opponent's sword and your sword are locked together and you strike as strongly as possible without raising your sword at all. One must strike quickly, exerting strength with the legs, torso, and hands.

This blow is hard to strike without repeated practice. If you cultivate it to perfection, it has a powerful impact.

THE CRIMSON FOLIAGE HIT

The idea of the crimson foliage hit is to knock the opponent's sword down and take the sword over. When an opponent is brandishing a sword before you, intending to strike, hit, or catch, you strike the opponent's sword strongly, your striking mood that of "striking without thought and without form," or even "spark hitting." When you then follow up closely on that, striking with the sword tip downward (*kissakisagari*), your opponent's sword will inevitably fall.

If you cultivate this blow to perfection, it is easy to knock a sword down. It must be well practiced.

The Body Instead of the Sword

The body in this sense can also be called the body that takes the place of the sword. In general, when you take the offensive, your sword and your body are not launched simultaneously. Depending on your chances of striking the opponent, you first adopt an offensive posture with your body, and your sword strikes independently of your body.

Sometimes you may strike with your sword without your body stirring, but generally the body goes on the offensive first, followed up by the stroke of the sword. This requires careful observation and practice.

Striking and Hitting

By *striking* and *hitting*, I mean two different things. The sense of *striking* is that whatever stroke you employ, you make a deliberate and certain strike. Hitting means something like running into someone. Even if you hit an opponent so hard that he dies on the spot, this is a hit. A strike is when you consciously and deliberately strike the blow you intend to strike. This requires examination and reflection.

To hit an opponent on the hands or legs means to hit first, in order to make a powerful strike after hitting. To hit means something like "feel out." If you really learn to master this, it is something extraordinary. It takes work.

THE BODY OF THE SHORT-ARMED MONKEY

The posture of the short-armed monkey means not reaching out with your hand. The idea is that when you close in on an opponent, you get in there quickly, before the opponent strikes, without putting forth a hand at all.

When you intend to reach forth, your body invariably pulls back; so the idea is to move the whole body quickly to get inside the opponent's defense. It is easy to get in from arm's length. This should be investigated carefully.

THE STICKY BODY

The sticky body means getting inside and sticking fast to an opponent. When you get inside the opponent's defenses, you stick tight with your head, body, and legs. The average person gets his head and legs in quickly, but the body shrinks back. Sticking to an opponent means that you stick so close that there is no gap between your bodies. This should be investigated carefully.

COMPARING HEIGHT

Comparing height means that when you close in on an opponent, under whatever circumstances, you extend your legs, waist, and neck, so that your body does not contract; closing in powerfully, you align your face with the opponent's, as if you were comparing height and proving to be the taller of the two. The essential point is to maximize your height and close in strongly. This requires careful work.

GLUING

When your opponent and you both strike forth, and your opponent catches your blow, the idea is to close in with your sword glued to the opponent's sword. Gluing means that the sword is hard to get away from; you should close in without too much force. Sticking to the opponent's sword as if glued, when you move in close it does not matter how quietly you move in.

There is gluing and there is leaning. Gluing is stronger than leaning. These things must be distinguished.

THE BODY BLOW

The body blow is when you close in on an opponent's side and hit him with your body. Turning your face slightly to the side and thrusting your left shoulder forward, you hit him in the chest.

In making the hit, exert as much strength as possible with your body; in making the hit, the idea is to close in with a bound at the moment of peak tension.

Once you have learned to close in like this, you can knock an opponent several yards back. It is even possible to hit an opponent so hard that he dies.

This requires thorough training and practice.

THREE PARRIES

When you attack an opponent, in order to parry the blow of the opponent's sword, making as if to stab him in the eyes, you dash his sword to your right with your sword, thus parrying it.

There is also what is called the stabbing parry. Making as if to stab the opponent in the right eye, with the idea of clipping off his neck, you parry the opponent's striking sword with a stabbing thrust.

Also, when an opponent strikes and you close in with a shorter sword, without paying so much attention to the parrying sword, you close in as if to hit your opponent in the face with your left hand.

These are the three parries. Making your left hand into a fist, you should think of it as if you were punching your opponent in the face. This is something that requires thorough training and practice.

STABBING THE FACE

When you are even with an opponent, it is essential to keep thinking of stabbing him in the face with the tip of your sword in the intervals between the opponent's sword blows and your own sword blows. When you have the intention of stabbing your opponent in the face, he will try to get both his face and his body out of the way. When you can get your opponent to shrink away, there are various advantages of which you can avail yourself to win. You should work this out thoroughly.

In the midst of battle, as soon as an opponent tries to get out of the way, you have already won. Therefore it is imperative not to forget about the tactic of "stabbing the face." This should be cultivated in the course of practicing martial arts.

STABBING THE HEART

Stabbing the heart is used when fighting in a place where there is no room for slashing, either overhead or to the sides, so you stab the opponent. To make the opponent's sword miss you, the idea is to turn the ridge of your sword directly toward your opponent, drawing it back so that the tip of the sword does not go off kilter, and thrusting it into the opponent's chest.

This move is especially for use when you are tired out, or when your sword will not cut. It is imperative to be able to discern expertly.

THE CRY

A cry and a shout are used whenever you launch an attack to overcome an opponent and the opponent also strikes back; coming up from below as if to stab the opponent, you strike a counterblow.

In any case, you strike with a cry and a shout in rapid succession. The idea is to thrust upward with a cry, then strike with a shout.

This move is one that can be used anytime in a duel. The way to cry and shout is to raise the tip of the sword with the sense of stabbing, then slashing all at once, immediately upon bringing it up. The rhythm must be practiced well and examined carefully.

The Slapping Parry

When you are exchanging blows with an opponent in a duel, you hit the opponent's sword with your own sword as he strikes; this is called the slapping parry. The idea of the slapping parry is not to hit particularly hard, nor to catch and block; responding to the opponent's striking sword, you hit the striking sword, then immediately strike the opponent.

It is essential to be the first to hit and the first to strike. If the rhythm of your parrying blow is right, no matter how powerfully an opponent strikes, as long as you have any intention at all of hitting, your sword tip will not fall. This must be learned by practice and carefully examined.

A STAND AGAINST MANY OPPONENTS

A stand against many opponents is when an individual fights against a group. Drawing both long and short swords, you hold them out to the left and right, extending them horizontally. The idea is that even if opponents come at you from all four sides, you chase them into one place.

Discerning the order in which opponents attack, deal with those who press forward first; keeping an eye on the whole picture, determining the stands from which opponents launch their attacks, swinging both swords at the same time without mutual interference, it is wrong to wait. The idea is to immediately adopt the ready position with both swords out to the sides and, when an opponent comes forth, to cut in with a powerful attack, overpower him, then turn right away to the next one to come forth and slash him down.

Intent on herding opponents into a line, when they seem to be doubling up, sweep right in powerfully, not allowing a moment's gap.

It will be hard to make headway if you only chase opponents around en masse. Then again, if you think about getting them one after another as they come forth, you will have a sense of waiting and so will also have a hard time making headway. The thing is to win by sensing the opponents' rhythms and knowing where they break down.

If you get a group of practitioners together from time to time and learn how to corner them, it is possible to take on one opponent, or ten, or even twenty opponents, with peace of mind. It requires thorough practice and examination.

Advantage in Dueling

Advantage in dueling means understanding how to win using the long sword according to the laws of martial arts. This cannot be written down in detail; one must realize how to win by practice. This is the use of the long sword that reveals the true science of martial arts; it is transmitted by word of mouth.

The Single Stroke

This means to gain victory with certainty by the accuracy of a single stroke. This cannot be comprehended without learning martial arts well. If you practice this well, you will master martial arts, and this will be a way to attain victory at will. Study carefully.

THE STATE OF DIRECT PENETRATION

The mind of direct penetration is something that is transmitted when one receives the true path of the school of Two Swords. It is essential to practice well, so as to train the body to this military science. This is transmitted orally.

EPILOGUE

The above is an overall account of the arts of swordsmanship in my individual school, which I have recorded in this scroll.

In military science, the way to learn how to take up the long sword and gain victory over others starts with using the five formal techniques to learn the five kinds of guard position, then learning how to wield a long sword and gain total freedom of movement, sharpening the mind to discern the rhythms of the path, and taking up the sword oneself. When you are able to maneuver your body and feet however you wish, you beat one person, you beat two people, and you come to know what is good and what is bad in martial arts.

Studying and practicing each item in this book, fighting with opponents, you gradually attain the principles of the science; keeping it in mind at all times, without any sense of hurry, learning its virtues whenever the opportunity arises, taking on any and all opponents in duels, learning the heart of the science, even though it is a path of a thousand miles, you walk one step at a time.

Thinking unhurriedly, understanding that it is the duty of warriors to practice this science, determine that today you will overcome your self of the day before, tomorrow you will win over those of lesser skill, and later you will win over those of greater skill. Practicing in accord with this book, you should determine not to let your mind get sidetracked.

No matter how many opponents you beat, as long as you do anything in contravention of training, it cannot be the true path. When this principle comes to mind, you should understand how to overcome even dozens of opponents all by yourself. Once you can do that, you should also be able to grasp the principles of large-scale and individual military science by means of the power of knowledge of the art of the sword.

This is something that requires thorough examination, with a thousand days of practice for training and ten thousand days of practice for refinement.

The Fire Scroll

IN THE MILITARY SCIENCE of the individual Two Sword school, combat is thought of as fire. Matters pertaining to victory and defeat in combat are thought of as a scroll of fire and so are written down herein.

To begin with, people of the world all think of the principles of advantage in martial arts in small terms. Some know how to take advantage of a flick of the wrist, using the tips of the fingers. Some know how to win using a fan, by a timely movement of the forearm. Then again, using a bamboo sword or something like that, they may just learn the minor advantage of speed, training their hands and feet in this way, concentrating on trying to take advantage of a little more speed.

As far as my military science is concerned, I have discerned the principles of living and dying through numerous duels in which I set my life on the line, learning the science of the sword, getting to know the strength and weakness of opponents' sword blows, comprehending the uses of the blade and ridge of the sword, and practicing how to kill opponents. In the course of doing this, little sissy things never even occurred to me. Especially when one is in full combat gear, one does not think of small things.

Furthermore, to fight even five or ten people singlehandedly in duels with your life on the line and find a sure way to beat them is what my military science is all about. So what is the difference between the logic of one person beating ten people and a thousand people beating ten thousand people? This is to be given careful consideration.

Nevertheless, it is impossible to collect a thousand or ten thousand people for everyday practice to learn this science. Even if you are exercising alone with a sword, assess the knowledge and tactics of all adversaries, know the strong and weak moves of adversaries, find out how to beat everyone by means of the knowledge and character of military science, and you will become a master of this path.

Who in the world can attain the direct penetration of my military science? Training and refining day and night with the determination to eventually consummate it, after having perfected it, one gains a unique freedom, spontaneously attains wonders, and is endowed with inconceivable powers of penetration. This is how cosmic law is carried out through martial arts.

THE PHYSICAL SITUATION

In discerning the lay of the physical situation, there is what is known as positioning yourself with the sun at your back. This means that you take up your stance with the sun behind you. If the situation does not allow you to keep the sun at your back, then you should strive to keep the sun to your right.

This also applies indoors, where you should keep the light to your back, or to your right. It is desirable to be sure that there is nothing in the way behind you, and that there is plenty of room to your left, taking a stance in such a way as to cut off the space to your right and close in.

At night also, where you can see your opponents, take your stand with fires to your back and lights to your right, as indicated above.

In order to "look down on the enemy,"

understand that you should take your stand on the highest ground, even if it is only slightly elevated. Indoors, the seat of honor should be regarded as the high ground.

Anyway, when it comes to battle, the idea is to chase opponents to your left; it is essential to make sure that obstacles are to the rear of your opponents, then chase them into an obstacle any way you can.

When you get opponents to an obstacle, in order to prevent them from observing the situation, press your attack without letup so that they cannot look around. The same thing about not letting opponents observe the situation also applies indoors, when you are chasing them into doorsills, head jambs, doors, screens, verandas, pillars, or other obstacles.

In any case, the direction in which you chase opponents should be toward places where the footing is bad or there is obstruction on either side. Use whatever qualities of the setting you can, concentrating on taking advantage of the situation. This is something that calls for careful and thorough reflection and practice.

THREE PREEMPTIONS

There are three kinds of preemption. One is when you preempt by attacking an opponent on your own initiative; this is called preemption from a state of suspension. Another is when you preempt an opponent making an attack on you; this is called preemption from a state of waiting. Yet another is when you and an opponent attack each other simultaneously; this is called preemption in a state of mutual confrontation.

These are the three ways of preemption. At the beginning of any battle, there are no other choices but these three initiatives. Since it is a matter of gaining victory quickly by preemption, therefore preemption is the foremost concern in martial arts.

There are many details involved in preemption, but they cannot be fully written down because it is a matter of putting priority on the pattern of the particular time, perceiving the intention of opponents, and using your knowledge of martial arts to win.

First there is preemption from a state of suspension. When you want to attack, you remain calm and quiet, then get the jump on your opponent by attacking suddenly and quickly. You can preempt by being outwardly powerful and swift while inwardly leaving reserves. You can also get the jump by steeling your mind to the utmost, accelerating your pace a bit, and making a violent attack the instant you get up close to the opponent. You can also win by letting your mind go free, determining to beat your opponent at the same thing from start to finish, gaining victory by thoroughgoing strength of heart. All of these are examples of preemption from a state of suspension.

Second is preemption from a state of waiting. When an opponent comes at you, you do not react but appear to be weak: then, when the opponent gets near, you spring away with a powerful leap, almost as if you were flying; then, when you see the opponent slack, you forcefully overcome him straightaway. This is one way of preemption. Also, when an opponent attacks and you aggressively meet the attack, the moment you sense a change in the rhythm of the opponent's attack, you can gain victory right then and there. This is the principle of preemption from a state of waiting.

Third is preemption in a state of mutual confrontation. In case an opponent attacks swiftly, you attack calmly yet powerfully; when the opponent gets close, tighten your bearing with absolute resolve, and when the opponent shows signs of slacking, overcome him with force immediately. Then again, when an opponent attacks calmly and quietly, accelerate your own attack slightly, with your body lightly buoyant; when the opponent gets close, clash once and then, adapting to his condition, overcome him forcefully. This is preemption in a state of mutual confrontation.

These moves are hard to write about in detail; they should be worked out along the general lines of the moves written down here. These three ways of preemption depend on the time and logic of the situation. Even though you are not to be always the one to attack, if it amounts to the same thing, you would rather take the initiative and put opponents on the defensive.

However it may be, the idea of preemption is gaining certain victory through the power of knowledge of martial arts. It must be cultivated and refined very thoroughly.

HOLDING DOWN THE PILLOW

Holding down the pillow means not letting someone raise his head. In martial arts, in the course of dueling, it is bad to be maneuvered around by others. It is desirable to maneuver opponents around freely, by whatever means you may.

Therefore opponents will be thinking along these lines, and you too have this intention, but it is impossible to succeed in this without comprehending what others are doing.

Martial arts include stopping an opponent's striking blows, arresting his thrusts, tearing away his grips. Holding down the pillow means that when you have attained my science in reality and are engaged with an opponent, whenever the opponent evinces any sign of intending to make a move, you perceive it before he acts. Stopping an opponent's attack at the initial outset, not letting him follow through, is the sense of "holding down the pillow."

For example, you inhibit an opponent's attack from the letter *a*, so to speak; you inhibit an opponent's leap from the letter *l*, and inhibit an opponent's cut from the letter *c*. These are all the same idea.

Whenever opponents try to attack you, let them go ahead and do anything that is useless, while preventing them from doing anything useful. This is essential to military science.

Here, if you consciously try to thwart

opponents, you are already late. First, doing whatever you do scientifically, thwart the opponent's very first impulse to try something, thus foiling everything. To manipulate opponents in this way is mastery of the art of war, which comes from practice. The act of holding down the pillow requires thorough examination.

CROSSING A FORD

When you cross a sea, there are places called straits. Also, places where you cross a sea even twelve or fifteen miles wide are called fords. In going through the human world as well, in the course of a lifetime there will be many points that could be called crossing a ford.

On the sea-lanes, knowing where the fords are, knowing the state of the boat, knowing the weather, even without launching companion boats, you adapt to the state of the time, sometimes taking advantage of crosswinds, sometimes even getting favorable winds, knowing that even if the wind changes you can still reach port by oar, you take command of the ship and cross the ford.

With that attitude, in passing through the human world you should also have a sense of crossing a ford in an emergency.

In martial arts, in the midst of battle, it is also essential to "cross the ford." Sensing the state of opponents, aware of your own mastery, you cross the ford by means of the appropriate principles, just as a skilled captain goes over a sea-lane.

Having crossed over the ford, furthermore, there is peace of mind.

To "cross a ford," put the adversary in a weak position and get the jump yourself; then you will generally quickly prevail. Whether in large-scale military science or individual martial arts, the sense of crossing a ford is essential. It should be savored thoroughly.

KNOWING THE STATE OF AFFAIRS

In large-scale military science, knowing the state of affairs means discerning the flourishing and decline of opponents, discerning the intentions of adversary troops and perceiving their condition, clearly seeing the state of affairs, determining how to deploy your own troops so as to gain certain victory by the principles of military science, and doing battle with knowledge of what lies ahead.

Also, in individual martial arts, you determine opponents' traditions, observe the personal character of adversaries, find out people's strengths and weaknesses, maneuver in ways contrary to opponents' expectations, determine opponents' highs and lows, ascertain the rhythms in between, and make the first move; this is essential.

If your own power of insight is strong, the state of affairs of everything will be visible to you. Once you have attained complete independent mastery of martial arts, you will be able to figure out the minds of opponents and thus find many ways to win. This demands work.

STOMPING A SWORD

Stomping a sword is a move used only in martial arts. First of all, in large-scale military science, even with bows and guns, when opponents attack you with whatever they have, after they have shot their first volley and are renewing their barrage, it is hard for you to make your attack if you are cocking a bow or loading a gun. The idea is to attack quickly while the enemy is in the process of shooting.

The sense of this is that if you attack quickly, it is hard to use arrows against you, hard to shoot you with a gun. The idea is that whatever opponents attack with, you immediately sense the pattern and gain victory by stomping down anything the opponent does.

In the context of individual martial arts as well, if you strike in the wake of an opponent's striking sword, it will turn into a clashing, clanging volley of blows, and you will get nowhere. When an opponent lashes out with his sword, you overpower his assault by stomping the sword down with your foot, seeing to it that he cannot strike a second blow.

Stomping is not only done with the feet. You should also learn to "stomp" with your body, "stomp" with your mind, and of course "stomp" with a sword, in such a way as to prevent opponents from making a second move.

This means getting the jump on everything. It does not mean randomly hitting an opponent with the idea of settling the contest all at once. It means instantaneous and unyielding follow-up. This should be investigated thoroughly.

KNOWING DISINTEGRATION

Disintegration is something that happens to everything. When a house crumbles, a person crumbles, or an adversary crumbles, they fall apart by getting out of rhythm with the times.

In large-scale military science, it is also essential to find the rhythm of opponents as they come apart and pursue them so as not to let openings slip by. If you miss the timing of vulnerable moments, there is the likelihood of counterattack.

In individual martial arts it also happens that an adversary will get out of rhythm in combat and start to fall apart. If you let such a chance get by you, the adversary will recover and thwart you. It is essential to follow up firmly on any loss of poise on the part of an opponent, to prevent him from recovering.

The follow-up calls for directness and power; it is a matter of lashing out violently in such a way that an opponent cannot recover. This lashing out must be carefully analyzed. If you do not let go, there is a sense of slovenliness. This is something that requires work.

BECOMING THE OPPONENT

Becoming the opponent means you should put yourself in an opponent's place and think from the opponent's point of view.

As I see the world, if a burglar holes up in a house, he is considered a powerful opponent. From his point of view, however, the whole world is against him; he is holed up in a helpless situation. The one who is holed up is a pheasant; the one who goes in there to fight it out is a hawk. This calls for careful reflection.

In large-scale military science as well, opponents are thought of as powerful and dealt with carefully. When you have good troops, know the principles of martial arts well, and sense the way to overcome an opponent, you need not worry.

You should also put yourself in the opponent's position in individual martial arts. When one meets a master of the science, someone who comprehends martial arts and is good at the science, one thinks one will lose. Consider this well.

Letting Go Four Hands

Letting go four hands is for when you and an opponent are in a deadlock and no progress is being made in the fight. It means that when you think you are going to get into a deadlock, you stop that right away and seize victory by taking advantage of a different approach.

In large-scale military science as well, if there is total deadlock and no progress is being made, there will be a loss of personnel. It is essential to stop right away and seize victory by taking advantage of a tactic unsuspected by the enemy.

In individual martial arts also, if you think you are getting into a deadlock, then it is essential to immediately change your approach, ascertain the opponent's state, and determine how to win by means of a very different tactic.

MOVING SHADOWS

Moving shadows is something you do when you cannot discern what an adversary is thinking.

In large-scale military science, when you cannot discern the enemy's state, you pretend to make a powerful attack to see what they will do. Having seen opponents' methods, it is easy to seize victory by taking advantage of different tactics specially adapted to each case.

In individual martial arts also, when an opponent is brandishing his sword behind him or to his side, when he is suddenly about to strike, he shows his intent in his sword. Once it shows perceptibly, you should immediately sense the advantage and know how to win with certainty. If you are inattentive, you will miss the rhythm. This should be examined thoroughly.

ARRESTING SHADOWS

Arresting shadows is something you do when adversaries' aggressive intentions toward you are perceptible.

In large-scale military science, this means to arrest the enemy's action at the point of the very impulse to act. If you demonstrate strongly to opponents how you control the advantage, they will change their minds, inhibited by this strength. You change your attitude too— to an empty mind, from which you take the initiative and seize victory.

In individual martial arts as well, you use an advantageous rhythm to arrest the powerful determination of the adversary's motivation; then you find the winning advantage in the moment of pause and now take the initiative. This must be worked out thoroughly.

INFECTION

There is infection in everything. Even sleepiness can be infectious, and yawning can be infectious. There is even the infection of a time.

In large-scale military science, when adversaries are excited and evidently are in a hurry to act, you behave as though you are completely unfazed, giving the appearance of being thoroughly relaxed and at ease. Do this, and adversaries themselves are influenced by this mood, becoming less enthusiastic.

When you think opponents have caught that mood, you empty your own mind and act quickly and firmly, thus to gain the winning advantage.

In individual martial arts as well, it is essential to be relaxed in body and mind, notice the moment an opponent slackens, and quickly take the initiative to win.

There is also something called "entrancing" that is similar to infection. One entrancing mood is boredom. Another is restlessness. Another is faintheartedness. This should be worked out thoroughly.

UPSET

Upset happens in all sorts of things. One way it happens is through a feeling of being under acute pressure. Another is through a feeling of unreasonable strain. A third is through a feeling of surprise at the unexpected.

In large-scale military science, it is essential to cause upset. It is critical to attack resolutely where enemies are not expecting it; then, while their minds are unsettled, use this to your advantage to take the initiative and win.

In individual martial arts also, you appear relaxed at first, then suddenly charge powerfully; as the opponent's mind changes pitch, it is essential that you follow what he does, not letting him relax for a moment, perceiving the advantage of the moment and discerning right then and there how to win. This must be investigated diligently.

THREAT

There is fright in everything. This means being frightened by the unexpected.

Even in large-scale military science, threatening an adversary is not something right before the eyes. You may threaten by sound, you may threaten by making the small seem large, and you may threaten by making an unexpected move from the side. These are situations in which fright occurs. If you can seize the moment of fright, you can take advantage of it to gain victory.

In individual martial arts also, you can threaten by means of your body, you can threaten by means of your sword, and you can threaten by means of your voice. What is essential is to suddenly make a move totally unexpected by the opponent, pick up on the advantage of fright, and seize victory right then and there. This must be worked out thoroughly.

STICKING TIGHT

Sticking tight means when you are fighting at close range, you and your adversary each exerting great force against the other, and you see that it is not going well, you then stick tight to your opponent; the essential point is to take advantage of opportunities to win even as you wrestle together.

Whether in large- or small-scale military science, when you and opponents have taken sides and are facing off and it is not clear who will prevail, right then and there you stick tight to the opponents, so that you cannot be separated, and in that process find the advantage, determine how to win, and seize victory powerfully; this is quintessential. This must be studied diligently.

COMING UP AGAINST CORNERS

Coming up against corners means that when you push something that is strong, it hardly gives way immediately, just like that.

In large-scale military science, observe the opposing troops; where they have surged ahead, hit the corner of this strong front, and you should get the advantage.

As the corner collapses, everyone gets the feeling of collapse. Even as they are collapsing, it is essential to realize when each corner is ready to go and sense when to overcome it.

In individual martial arts too, when you inflict pain on part of his body each time an opponent makes an aggressive move, his body will weaken by degrees until he is ready to collapse and it is easy to beat him.

It is essential to study this carefully to discern where you can win.

FLUSTERING

Flustering opponents means acting in such a way as to prevent them from having a steady mind.

In large-scale military science, this means that you assess adversaries' minds on the battlefield and use the power of your knowledge of the art of war to manipulate their attention, making them think confusing thoughts about what you are going to do. It means finding a rhythm that will fluster adversaries, accurately discerning where you can win.

In individual martial arts as well, you try various maneuvers according to the opportunity of the moment, making the opponent think you are now going to do this, now that, now something else, until you find the opponent starting to get flustered, and thus you win at will. This is the essence of battle; it should be studied very carefully.

THREE SHOUTS

The three shouts are called the initial, middle, and final shout. The essential point is to call out in accord with the situation. Because a shout is forceful, we shout in emergencies like fires and squalls; the voice shows force and power.

In large-scale military science, at the

beginning of battle the shouting should be as loud as possible, in the course of battle the shouting should be low-pitched and booming from the depths, while after victory the shouting should be loud and strong. These are the three shouts.

In individual martial arts, you feint and shout in order to stir the opponent, then lash out after your cry. You also shout after having struck an opponent down, with a cry signaling victory. These are called before and after shouts.

You never shout at the same time as you swing your sword. When you shout in the midst of battle, you use the sound to mount a rhythm, crying out in a low pitch.

MIXING

In the context of large-scale combat, mixing means that when two groups are facing off and your opponents are strong, you attack one of the opponents' flanks, as if to mix in with them; then, when you see the opponents crumble, you leave off and attack again where they are strong. In general, the idea is to attack in a winding zigzag.

This is also essential in the context of individual martial arts, when you face a group of adversaries singlehandedly. Each time you have finished one off or driven one off, again you attack a strong one, finding the opponents' rhythm, zigzagging left and right in a suitable rhythm, observing the condition of the adversary so as to attack effectively.

When you have found an enemy's range and are going to cut through, the principle of the advantage is to seize victory forcefully, without any reservations. This state of mind also applies to a situation when you are closing in on a powerful opponent in individual combat.

The sense of mixing is to plunge right in without any hesitation in your steps. This should be distinguished carefully.

CRUSHING

Crushing requires a crushing mood, as when you view an opponent as weak and become strong yourself, thus overwhelming your adversary.

In large-scale military science, this means you look down upon an enemy whose numbers are small, or even if there are many of them, when opponents are demoralized and weakening, you concentrate your force on crushing them, thus mowing them down.

If your crushing is weak, it can backfire. You have to carefully distinguish the state of mind in which you are fully in control as you crush.

In the context of individual martial arts too, when your opponent is not as skilled as you are, or when his rhythm is fouled up, or when he starts to back off, it is essential not to let him catch his breath. Mow him right down without even giving him time to blink his eyes. The most important thing is not to let him recover.

This should be studied very carefully.

MOUNTAIN AND SEA CHANGING

"Mountain and sea" means that it is bad to do the same thing over and over again. You may have to repeat something once, but it should not be done a third time.

When you try something on an opponent, if it does not work the first time, you will not get any benefit out of rushing to do it again. Change your tactics abruptly, doing something completely different. If that still does not work, then try something else.

Thus the science of martial arts involves the presence of mind to act as the sea when the enemy is like a mountain, and act as a mountain when the enemy is like a sea. This requires careful reflection.

KNOCKING THE HEART OUT

When you fight with an adversary and appear to win by your skill in this science, your opponent may still have ideas and, while appearing to be beaten, still inwardly refuse to acknowledge defeat. Knocking the heart out is for such cases.

This means that you suddenly change your attitude to stop the enemy from entertaining any such ideas; so the main thing is to see that adversaries feel defeated from the bottom of their hearts.

You can knock the heart out of people

with weapons or with your body or with your mind. It is not to be understood in just one way.

When your enemies have completely lost heart, you do not have to pay attention to them anymore. Otherwise, you remain mindful. As long as adversaries still have ambitions, they will hardly collapse.

In both large- and small-scale martial arts, knocking the heart out should be practiced thoroughly.

BECOMING NEW

When fighting with enemies, if you get to feeling snarled up and are making no progress, you toss your mood away and think in your heart that you are starting everything anew. As you get the rhythm, you discern how to win. This is "becoming new."

Anytime you feel tension and friction

building up between yourself and others, if you change your mind that very moment, you can prevail by the advantage of radical difference. This is "becoming new."

In large-scale military science, it is essential to understand becoming new. It is something that suddenly appears through the power in knowledge of martial arts. This must be well considered.

SMALL AND LARGE

When you are fighting adversaries and get to feeling snarled up in petty maneuvers, remember this rule of military science: while in the midst of minutiae, suddenly you shift to a large perspective.

Changing to great or small is an intentional part of the science of the art of war. It is essential for warriors to seek this even in the ordinary consciousness of human life. This mentality is critical to military science, whether large or small scale.

This concern should be given careful consideration.

A COMMANDER KNOWING SOLDIERS

"A commander knowing soldiers" is a method always practiced in times of conflict after having reached the mastery to which one aspires. Having attained the power in the knowledge of the arts of war, you think of your adversaries as your own soldiers, understanding that you should do with them as you wish, intending to manipulate them freely. You are the commander, the opponents are the troops. This takes work.

Letting Go of the Hilt

"Letting go of the hilt" has various meanings. It has the meaning of winning without a sword, and it also has the meaning of failing to win with a sword. The various different senses cannot be written down but call for thorough training and practice.

Being Like a Rock Wall

"Being like a rock wall" is when a master of martial arts suddenly becomes like a rock wall, inaccessible to anything at all, immovable. This is transmitted by word of mouth.

Epilogue

What is written above consists entirely of things that constantly come to mind in the course of practicing the art of swordsmanship of my individual school. Because I am now writing these principles down for the first time, they are somewhat mixed up in terms of order, and it is hard to define them in detail. Nevertheless, they can be guidelines for people who are supposed to learn this science.

I have concentrated on martial arts since youth, training my hands and body to the mastery of swordsmanship, getting into all sorts of various states of mind. What I see on inquiry into other schools is that some are pretentious talkers, and some perform fancy manuevers with their hands; even though they may look good to people, there is surely no true heart there at all.

Of course, it may seem as if people are training body and mind even when they are practicing such things, but they become sicknesses of the path, persistent and hard to get rid of; they are bases of the decay of the straight path of martial arts in the world, and of the abandonment of the Way.

For the art of swordsmanship to be a real science, such as to win victory in battle with adversaries, no change whatsoever is to be made in these principles. When you attain the power of knowledge of my military science and put it into practice in a straightforward manner, there can be no doubt of victory.

The Wind Scroll

MILITARY SCIENCE involves knowledge of the methods of other schools. Here in this Wind Scroll, I have written about the various other schools of martial arts. Unless you know the ways of other schools, you certainly cannot understand the way of my individual school.

What I see on inquiry into others' martial arts is that some schools use large long swords and concentrate on power in their moves. Some practice their science using a short long sword they call a "little long sword." There are also schools that contrive many moves with the long sword, calling the positions of the sword the formal techniques and transmitting the science as the inner teaching.

In this scroll I will clearly expose the fact that none of these are the real Way, thus to let it be known what is good and what bad, what true and what false. The principle of my individual school is something distinctly different. Other schools become theatrical, dressing up and showing off to make a living, commercializing martial arts; therefore it would seem that they are not the true Way.

Furthermore, martial art is conventionally viewed in a limited way, as if it consisted only of swordsmanship. Do you think you have realized how to attain victory just by learning to wield a long sword and training your body and hands? This is not a certain way in any case.

I have exposed each of the deficiencies of other schools in this book. The point is to examine carefully and savor thoroughly, to come to an understanding of the advan-

tages of the individual school of Two
Swords.

ON WIELDING EXTRA-LONG SWORDS
IN OTHER SCHOOLS

There are some other schools that are fond
of extra-long swords. From the point of
view of my martial art, I see them as weak
schools. The reason for this is that these
other schools do not know about prevail-
ing over others by any means necessary;
considering the length of the sword its virtue, they must want their swords to be
extra long so that they can beat opponents
from a distance.

The conventional saying about winning
by even an inch in reach is something that
refers to people who know nothing about
martial arts. Therefore, to try to win from
a distance by an advantage in sword length
without knowing the principles of martial

arts is something that people do because of weakness of heart. That is why I consider this weak martial art.

At times when you are engaged with an opponent at close quarters, the longer your sword is, the harder it is to strike with it; you cannot swing the sword back and forth enough, and it becomes a burden. Then you are in a worse situation than someone wielding a small side-arm sword.

For those who prefer extra-long swords, they have their own reason, but it is logical for themselves alone; from the point of view of the real Way of the world, it is illogical. Will you necessarily lose if you use a shorter long sword and not an extra-long sword?

And suppose the physical situation is such that above, below, and/or the sides are blocked; or suppose the social situation is one where only side arms are worn; to wish for an extra-long sword under these conditions is a bad attitude, because it is to doubt the science of martial arts.

Furthermore, there are people who lack the requisite physical strength.

Since ancient times it has been said that the great includes the small, so it is not a matter of indiscriminately disliking length; it is a matter of disliking the attitude of bias in favor of length.

In the context of large-scale military science, an extra-long sword is a large contingent, a shorter one is a small contingent. Is a battle between a small contingent and a large contingent impossible? There are many examples of a small contingent winning over a large contingent. Thus in my individual school there is an aversion to a narrow, biased attitude. This calls for careful examination.

POWERFUL SWORD BLOWS IN OTHER SCHOOLS

There should be no such thing as strong sword blows or weak sword blows. A swing of a sword made with the intention to swing powerfully is rough, and you can hardly win by roughness alone.

Furthermore, if you slash with unreasonable force when you are going to kill someone, intending to deal a powerful blow of the sword, you will not be successful.

Even when you are making a test cut on a dummy or something, it is wrong to try deliberately to slash powerfully.

When facing an enemy in mortal combat, nobody thinks of striking weakly or powerfully. When one only thinks of killing the other, there is no sense of strength, and of course no sense of weakness; one only thinks of the death of the enemy.

If you hit someone else's sword strongly using an extra-powerful swing, it will turn out badly because of excessive force. If you hit someone else's sword forcefully, your own sword will be delayed.

So there is no such thing as a particularly powerful sword blow. Even in large-scale military science, if you have a powerful contingent wishing to gain a forceful victory in battle, the fact is that your opponent also has powerful people and wants to fight forcefully. In that respect, both are the same. When it comes to winning victory in everything, it is impossible to prevail without reason.

In my school, no consideration is given to anything unreasonable; the heart of the matter is to use the power of the knowledge of martial arts to gain victory any way you can. This must be worked out thoroughly.

The Use of Shorter Long Swords in Other Schools

To think of winning by means of a shorter long sword alone is not the true Way. Since ancient times long and short swords have been distinguished in terminology.

Physically powerful people can wield even a large long sword with ease, so there is no point in unreasonable fondness for a shorter sword. The reason for this is that spears and halberds are also carried to make use of their length. The idea that you are going to use a shorter long sword to cut through, plunge in, and seize an opponent in the interval between swings of his sword is biased and therefore wrong.

Furthermore, when you watch out for gaps, everything else is neglected, and there comes to be a sense of entanglement, which is to be avoided. And if you try to use a short weapon to penetrate the enemy's defense and take over, that will not be of any use when in the midst of numerous opponents.

Even if you think that what you gain from a shorter weapon is the ability to cut through a crowd, leap freely, and whirl around, in each case you are in a defensive mode of swordplay and are thus in a distracted state of mind. This is not a reliable way to go.

You might just as well chase people around in a powerful and straightforward manner, making people jump out of the way, contriving to throw them into confusion, taking the route that aims solely at certain victory.

This logic also applies to large-scale military science. All else being equal, you might as well take a large contingent, attack the enemy all of a sudden, and destroy them at once. This attitude is the focus of military science.

What people of the world ordinarily study when they practice martial arts is to parry, deflect, get away, and get through safely; therefore their minds are drawn by this method and wind up being maneuvered and manipulated by others. Since the Way of martial arts is direct and straightforward, the intent to stalk and overcome people rightly is essential. This should be considered carefully.

NUMEROUS SWORD STROKES IN OTHER SCHOOLS

When an excessive number of sword moves are taught, it must be to commercialize the art and impress beginners with knowledge of many moves with a sword. This attitude is to be avoided in military science.

The reason for this is that it is delusion to think that there are all sorts of ways of cutting people down. In the matter of cutting people down, there are no different ways in the world. Whether or not one is knowledgeable, and even if one is a woman or a child, there are not so many ways to strike and cut; if there are variants, they are no more than stabbing and slashing.

To begin with, since the point is killing, there is no reason for there to be a large number of ways to do it. Even so, depending on the situation, according to events, in cases where there is obstruction in the surroundings, such as above or to the sides, there have to be five positions so that there is a way to wield a sword without getting stuck.

To add anything else, things like cutting an opponent down with a twist of the hands, a twirl of the body, or a leap to a distance, are not the true way. To cut someone down, you cannot cut them down by twisting or twirling; these are useless things.

In my military science, it is essential that the physical aspect and the mental state both be simple and direct, gaining victory by causing opponents to strain distortedly and go off kilter, causing the hearts of adversaries to do the twisting and twirling. This should be examined carefully.

POSITIONS OF THE SWORD IN OTHER SCHOOLS

It is wrong to concentrate solely on the guard position of the sword. Whenever there are guard positions in the world, it must be when there are no opponents.

The reasoning behind this is that to set up standard rules as customary standards or current rules is not feasible in the course of actually contesting for victory.

The thing is to contrive to put the adversary at a disadvantage.

Whatever the point of reference, the adoption of a guard position has the sense of making use of immovability. To guard a castle, or to array a battle line in a defensive position, has the sense of being strong and unaffected even under attack; this is the normal meaning.

In the course of struggle for victory by military science, the thing is to concentrate on seizing the initiative and getting the jump on others in everything. The sense of a guard or defensive posture is that of awaiting the initiative. This should be worked out thoroughly.

In the course of struggle for victory by military science, you win by disrupting others' defenses, by making moves opponents do not expect, by confusing opponents, or irritating them, or scaring them, sensing the pattern of the rhythm when opponents get mixed up to seize victory. Thus there is an aversion to the defensive attitude involved in concern with guard positions. Therefore in my science there is what is called having a guard without a guard, meaning that one has a defense without being defensive.

In large-scale military science also, the main concern for a pitched battle is to learn how many troops the adversary has, note the lay of the battleground, know the state of your own troops, marshal their best qualities, rally them, and only then start to fight.

There is a totally different feeling in being attacked by others first than in attacking others yourself. The sense of being able to wield a sword well enough to catch and parry an opponent's blows is tantamount to taking your spear and halberd and sticking them in the ground as fence posts. When you are going to strike an adversary, in contrast, you can even pull up a fence post and use it as you would a spear or halberd. This is something that should be examined carefully.

THE FOCUS OF THE EYES IN OTHER SCHOOLS

The focus of the eyes depends on the school: there are those who fix their eyes on the opponent's sword, and there are also those who fix their eyes on the opponent's hands; there are those who fix their eyes on the opponent's face, and there are also those who fix their eyes on the opponent's feet, and so on. When you try to fix your eyes on some particular point, there is a sense of distraction, and this becomes what is known as an affliction in martial arts.

People playing football may not keep their eyes on the ball, yet they can still steal it away with a kick and dribble it around, because when one is thoroughly practiced in something, it is not necessary to look deliberately. In the arts of jugglers too, when they are practiced in the techniques, they can balance a door on the nose and juggle several swords at once, all without deliberately watching; since they are involved in practice all the time, they see what is going on spontaneously.

In the context of the science of martial arts as well, when you become familiar with each adversary, perceive the degree of seriousness of people's minds, and are able to practice the science effectively, you can see even the distance and speed of a sword. Generally speaking, the focus of the eyes in martial arts is on the hearts and minds of the people involved.

When it comes to large-scale military science, the eyes are also focused on the state of the opposing troops.

Of two ways of perception, observing and seeing, the observing eye is stronger, perceiving the heart and mind of the adversary, seeing the state of the situation, focusing the eyes broadly, perceiving the conditions for battle, perceiving the strength and weakness of the occasion, concentrating on seizing victory with precision.

Whether in large- or small-scale military science, there is no narrow focus of the vision. As I have already written, by finicky narrowness of focus, you forget about bigger things and get confused, thus letting certain victory escape you. This principle demands careful reflection and thorough practice.

FOOTWORK IN OTHER SCHOOLS

There are various ways of quick-stepping, such as those known as the floating step, the leaping step, the springing step, the stomping step, the crow step, and so on. From the point of view of my martial art, all of these seem deficient.

The reason why I dislike the floating step is that one's steps are in any case likely to become unsteady in battle, so the proper course is to stride as surely as possible.

The reason I do not like the leaping step is that there is a sense of excitement in the leaping and a sense of fixation on leaping. Since there is no reason to leap over and over again, a leaping step is bad.

Also, the springing step is ineffective because there is a sense of bounding. The stomping step is a passive stance and is especially objectionable.

Other than these, there are also various quick-steps such as the crow step.

Since you may engage opponents in marshes or swamps, or in mountains and rivers, or on rocky plains, or on narrow roads, depending on the place, there are situations in which it is impossible to leap and spring or to quick-step.

In my martial art, there is no change in footwork; it is just like walking along a road as usual. Following the rhythm of the opponent, finding the right physical position in conditions of both hurry and calm, the stride should be orderly, without slack or excess.

In large-scale military science as well, footwork is critical. The reason for this is that if you attack indiscriminately without knowing the intentions of your adversary, you will miss the rhythm and find it hard to win. Also, if you are striding calmly and do not notice when opponents are demoralized and crumbling, you will let victory elude you and will be unable to effect a quick settlement of the contest.

It is essential to perceive discouragement and crumbling, then overwhelm adversaries by not letting them relax for even a moment. This requires thorough training and practice.

THE USE OF SPEED IN OTHER SCHOOLS

In martial arts, speed is not the true Way. As far as speed is concerned, the question of fast or slow in anything derives from failure to harmonize with the rhythm.

When you master an art or science, your performance does not appear to be fast. For example, there are professional courier runners who travel a route of about fifteen miles; but even so, they do not run fast from morning to night. As for those who lack the training, even if they seem to run all day, they do not reach the goal.

In the art of the dance, if a poor singer accompanies the song of a skilled singer, there is a sense of lag, which results in haste. Also, when "Old Pine" is played on the drums, it is a quiet piece, but in this case too, someone who is unskilled will tend to fall behind or get ahead. And while "High Dunes" has a rapid tempo, it is wrong to perform it too fast.

As the saying goes, the fast one stumbles and fails to get there on time. Of course, being too slow and too late is also bad.

The performance of an expert seems relaxed but does not leave any gaps. The actions of trained people do not seem rushed. The principle of the Way can be known from these illustrations.

Speed is particularly bad in the context of the science of martial arts. The reasons for this are as follows. Here too, depending on the place, say for example in a bog, it is impossible to move and run fast. With a long sword, there is no such thing as killing with greater speed; unlike with a fan or short sword, if you try to cut quickly, you will not be able to cut at all. This calls for careful discernment.

In large-scale military science as well, the feeling of speed and hurry is bad. With the attitude of "holding down the pillow," there is no being slow.

Furthermore, when people speed rashly, it is essential for you to be the reverse, becoming calm and quiet, not being drawn in by them. The way to work on this state of mind requires training and practice.

The Esoteric and Exoteric in Other Schools

In the context of matters of martial arts, what is to be called exoteric, what is to be called esoteric? Depending on the art, there are esoteric transmissions of the ultimate realization that are passed on as inner oral traditions, but when it comes to the principle of dueling with opponents, it is not a matter of fighting exoterically and killing esoterically.

My way of teaching martial arts is to have beginners learn and practice those of the techniques that are easily mastered, first teaching them the principles that they will readily understand. As for those things that their minds have a hard time reaching, I observe the understanding of each individual, subsequently teaching them deeper principles gradually, step by step. Even so, since I generally make them learn such things as have actual relevance to addressing these matters, there is no such thing as a distinction between the esoteric and the exoteric.

So it is in the world, when you go into the depths of the mountains, if you want to go farther, you will again come out of the mountains. In any art or science, there is that for which secrecy or reserve is appropriate, and that which may well be spoken of openly. But when it comes to the principles of war, what is to be hidden, what is to be revealed?

Accordingly, in transmitting my science, I do not care for written pledges or articles of penalties. Observing the intellectual power of students, teaching them a straight path, having them abandon the bad aspects of the "five ways" or "six ways" of martial arts, so that they naturally enter into the real science of warriors, causing their minds to be free from doubt—this is the way I teach martial arts. Thorough training and practice are necessary.

EPILOGUE

In the preceding nine articles on the martial arts of other schools, where I have written their outlines in this Wind Scroll, although it is imperative to write clearly about each school, from the initiation to the inner lore, I do not make a point of writing the names of which particular secret of which particular school I am referring to.

The reason for this is that the views of each school, and the logic of each path, are realized differently according to the individual person, depending on the mentality; so even in the same school there are some slight differences of understanding. Thus for the sake of posterity I have not recorded the particular schools to which I refer.

Having divided the general run of other schools into nine categories, when we look from the point of view of the right way for the world, from the point of view of straightforward human reason, things such as preferences for extra-long or extra-short swords, preferences for force or yielding, concern with crudeness and fineness, are all biased paths; so even if I do not reveal them as the initiatory or inner lore of other schools, everybody should know about them.

In my individual school, there is no such thing as a distinction between initiatory and inner lore about the long sword. There is no such thing as the ultimate guard. It is only a matter of understanding its effective qualities in your heart and mind; this is what is essential to martial art.

The Scroll of Emptiness

I N WRITING ABOUT the science of martial arts of the individual school of Two Swords in the Scroll of Emptiness, the meaning of emptiness is that the realm where nothing exists, or cannot be known, is seen as empty.

Of course, emptiness does not exist. Knowing of nonexistence while knowing of existence is emptiness.

Wrongly viewed among people of the world, not understanding anything is itself considered emptiness. This is not real emptiness; it is all delusion.

In the context of this science of martial arts as well, in carrying out the way as a warrior, not knowing the laws of warriors is not emptiness; being confused, one may call a state of helplessness emptiness, but this is not real emptiness.

Warriors learn military science accurately and go on to practice the techniques of martial arts diligently. The way that is practiced by warriors is not obscure in the least. Without any confusion in mind, without slacking off at any time, polishing the mind and attention, sharpening the eye that observes and the eye that sees, one should know real emptiness as the state where there is no obscurity and the clouds of confusion have cleared away.

As long as they do not know the real Way, whether in Buddhism or in worldly matters, everybody may think their path is sure and is a good thing, but from the point of view of the straight way of mind, seen in juxtaposition with overall social standards, they turn away from the true Way by the personal biases in their minds and the individual warps in their vision.

Knowing that mentality, taking straightforwardness as basic, taking the real mind as the Way, practicing martial arts in the broadest sense, thinking correctly, clearly, and comprehensively, taking emptiness as the Way, you see the Way as emptiness.

In emptiness there is good but no evil. Wisdom exists, logic exists, the Way exists, mind is empty.

12 May 1645

NOTES

1 *Two Skies* is one name for Musashi's school of martial arts, which he referred to as the individual school of Two Skies or Two Swords.

1 *Kannon* is one of the most popular of Buddhist icons, representing the activity of universal compassion. Kannon happened to be the icon of the temple where Musashi went into retreat; there is no indication that he had any particular devotion to Kannon.

6 *The Kashima and Kantori shrines* in eastern Japan were dedicated to war. The Kashima Shrine propitiates the god Takemikazuchi-no-mikoto, worshiped as a god of war since ancient times. The cult of this shrine was important in the early Japanese conquest of the largest of the islands in antiquity. The

Kashima New School of Accuracy, a school of martial arts associated with this shrine, was said to have been founded in the time of the prehistorical sixteenth emperor, Nintoku Tennō, who built Mozunomimi-hara-no-naka-no-misasagi, the largest mound tomb in the world. The Kashima New School of Accuracy is attributed to an ancient descendant of the god Kuninatsu-o-o-kashima-no-mikoto. The Ka(n)tori Shrine propitiates the god Futsunushi-no-kami. This shrine is reputed to have been established in the time of Jimmu Tennō, the first emperor of Japan, whose name Jimmu means Divine Warrior. A school of martial arts called the Katori Shinto School, or the Katori School of the Divine Sword (the two names are homonyms), was founded as recently as 1940.

44 *Five Kinds of Guard.* The word for "guard," *kamae,* comes from the verb *kamaeru,* which means to build, set up, adopt a (usually defensive) stance, posture, or attitude.

In social parlance, when someone *kamaeru*, that means the person becomes defensive in attitude. The related verb *kamau* means to take trouble over someone or something, to make a fuss.

97 *Infection.* The great pianist Josef Hofmann taught that a performer should convey excitement to an audience by means of the performer's memory of excitement, not by actually becoming excited oneself. This is a sublime example of the principle of infection.

97 *The infection of a time.* The mentality or mood of a time or an era dominates more effectively by infection than it could by overt persuasion or coercion, because the source and nature of the infection are not obvious.

138 *Five ways and six ways of martial arts.* Here Musashi refers to stylistic embellishment for its own sake, in contrast to the fundamental practicalities of the art of war.

BIBLIOGRAPHY

As Miyamoto Musashi emphasizes in his guidelines for students, martial artists in the Japanese warrior traditions were admonished to develop rounded mentalities and broad perceptions by studying cultural arts along with military science. The following books represent essential elements of East Asian martial and cultural traditions.

The Art of War. Translated by Thomas Cleary. Boston: Shambhala Publications, 1988. The most eminent Chinese classic of strategy, also studied by Japanese warriors.

The Book of Leadership and Strategy. Translated and edited by Thomas Cleary. Boston: Shambhala Publications, 1992. This book is a compendium of classical Taoist teachings, spiritual and cultural as well as political and martial.

The Essential Confucius. Translated and presented by Thomas Cleary. San Francisco: Harper San Francisco, 1992. The sayings of Confucius were regularly memorized in Japanese primary schools for centuries. Acquaintance with Confucius is absolutely indispensable for understanding the traditional fabric of East Asian societies.

The Japanese Art of War, by Thomas Cleary. Boston: Shambhala Publications, 1991. An analysis of the influences of martial rule on Japanese culture, including a discussion of the relationship between the ways of the warriors and Zen Buddhism.

Mastering the Art of War. Translated and edited by Thomas Cleary. Boston: Shambhala Publications, 1989. Illustrative elucidations of the principles of the classic *Art of War,* including war stories demonstrating tactics paralleling the work of Miyamoto Musashi.

Wen-tzu. Translated by Thomas Cleary. Boston: Shambhala Publications, 1991. Attributed to Lao-tzu, the *Wen-tzu* is one of the great classics of ancient Taoism, presenting teachings on the arts of strategy within the broader social and psychological context.

Zen Essence. Translated and edited by Thomas Cleary. Boston: Shambhala Publications, 1989. Fundamental Zen teachings and techniques presented by distinguished masters in easy conversational and discursive styles.

Zen Lessons. Translated by Thomas Cleary. Boston: Shambhala Publications, 1989. Precious documents from distinguished Zen masters describing and illustrating the social and psychological aspects of Zen Buddhism, both genuine and imitative.

LIBRARY OF CONGRESS
CATALOGING-IN-PUBLICATION DATA
Miyamoto, Musashi, 1584–1645.
[Gorin no sho. English]
The book of five rings/Miyamoto Musashi;
translated by Thomas Cleary.
p.   cm.—(Shambhala pocket classics)
Includes bibliographical references
ISBN-13 978-0-87773-998-2 (alk. paper)
ISBN-10 0-87773-998-6
1. MILITARY ART AND SCIENCE—EARLY WORKS TO
1800.
2. SWORDPLAY—JAPAN—EARLY WORKS TO 1800.
I. CLEARY, THOMAS F., 1949–   .
II. TITLE.   III. SERIES.
U101.M5913 1994   93-36271
355.5'47—dc20   CIP

(Continued on next page)